art and design

graphics

Chris Dunn

Hodder & Stoughton

A MEMBER OF THE HODDER HEADLINE GROUP

Introduction

Hilary Paynter, Stress, 1989, *wood engraving.*

You might like to find examples of illustrators' work. Children's story books often contain good examples. Choose an example and try your hand at designing a replacement page. A photocopier will help you to transfer the text.

The diversity of pictures on these two pages illustrates the wide variety of responses that can be made in the GCSE syllabus called Graphics. In the context of GCSE it contains such extremes as graphic design and the purely expressive work of some printmakers. This book deals firstly with the work of printmakers, showing the three main types of printmaking in use in schools. The work of the graphic designer is then examined. There are many types of work undertaken by the graphic designer and there are examples of some of these. Inevitably, with such a wide area to cover, there will be gaps.

The printmakers' prime concern is with the communication of ideas and feelings. They have this in common with the painter-sculptor; both create works of art in which the image is of more importance than its function. They use a wide range of techniques to produce their images, which are often in the form of editions of prints. These are usually printed by the artist. This enables the artist to subtly control and develop the quality of the print during its production.

There are, of course, exceptions. David Hockney (b. 1937) produced a limited (in number) edition of prints by commercial printing processes. Many artists have had silk-screened editions of prints produced by commercial printers. In the 1960s companies like Editions Alecto employed highly skilled printers just to work with artists on the production of prints. This had the effect of making original prints by modern artists available to a wider public.

Graphic designers work with an emphasis on communicating information. They usually work within a closely defined brief which tells them, often in great detail, what their work should contain. They use an enormous range of media. They work in illustration, advertising and presentation, indeed in any aspect of commercially printed material that needs it. Their work encompasses such extremes as pop-up card sculpture to detailed technical illustrations of subjects like the inside of the human body or the jet engine. Almost every aspect of the printed world around you has at some time been helped along its way by a graphic designer.

The wood engraving, *Stress* by Hilary Paynter, demonstrates the importance of creative ability as well as technical skill in the work of the illustrator.

These two frames (right) are from commercial films for Levi's jeans. The films have evolved through a complex process. The preparation of the idea or concept may have been the work of a graphic designer, the words might have been contributed by a copywriter, and the image, in this case, might have been produced by a photographer. This team approach, often under the control of an Art Director, is at the heart of the graphic design process.

Though not often used in schools lithography, like the example below, is a versatile print medium. Find out all you can about lithography and the great lithographers. In these three examples we see the whole range of graphic work described, from commercial design to emotive prints. The boundary area between the fine artist and the designer is mapped out here and, as in so many other areas, the most interesting examples can be found in this twilight area.

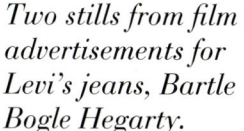

Two stills from film advertisements for Levi's jeans, Bartle Bogle Hegarty.

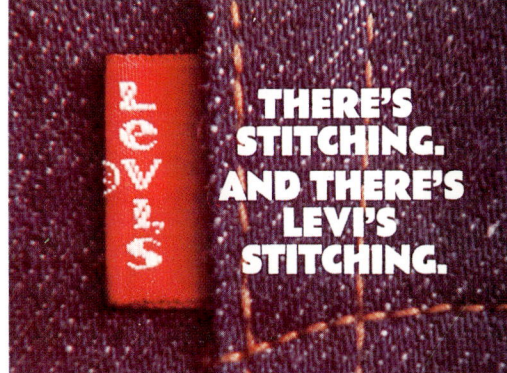

Ceri Richards (1903–1971), 'The force that through the green fuse drives the flower', from poems by Dylan Thomas, 1965, lithograph, 60 × 83 cm, Tate Gallery, London.

Looking at Printmaking

The photograph (below) is part of a series. The artist, Arnulf Ranier, has worked over it in oil pastel. The series is based on death masks of famous people. Through the process he tries to get closer to what he calls the 'secret of death'. By using the photograph as raw material, it draws close to an essential element in the work of a printmaker. It demonstrates the artist's ability to further develop the printed image.

Arnulf Ranier (b. 1929), Untitled Death Mask, 1978, *pastel on black and white photograph, 70 × 50.5 cm, Tate Gallery, London.*

Quite frequently artists are prepared to see the printed image as a stage on the way to a finished work, rather than as an end in itself. This can be seen in the desire to hand-colour prints either after printing or by carefully inking the plate during the printing process. In this way each print is subtly different. Often, especially with inexperienced artists, repeating identical images becomes an end in itself; prints that do not conform are rejected. Opportunities for creative work are lost. It 'freezes' the creative process. The identical image should be as a result of a conscious decision, not simply as a result of the capacities of the technique.

The plaster print (below) came from a block of plaster worked into while still damp. Only fine detail can be added when the plaster is dry. It can then be coated with ink and the raised surfaces will print. It is therefore called a relief or surface print. From a study of these two processes you can see that printmaking is not confined to traditional methods. Even though making a print can be a mechanical process it is still subject to the will of the artist before, during and after printing.

There are three basic printmaking techniques available in schools. These are not the only methods but they are the most usual. Relief or surface printing prints the areas that are left after the design has been cut away. Intaglio printing uses damp paper to take its print from the ink-filled lines that are cut out. Screen printing prints by forcing ink through a stencil. The next six pages explore these basic techniques through the work of some of the best exponents. This page demonstrates that these are not the only ways to print or even, in certain circumstances, the best. The only real limit is your imagination to adapt the techniques to do what you want them to.

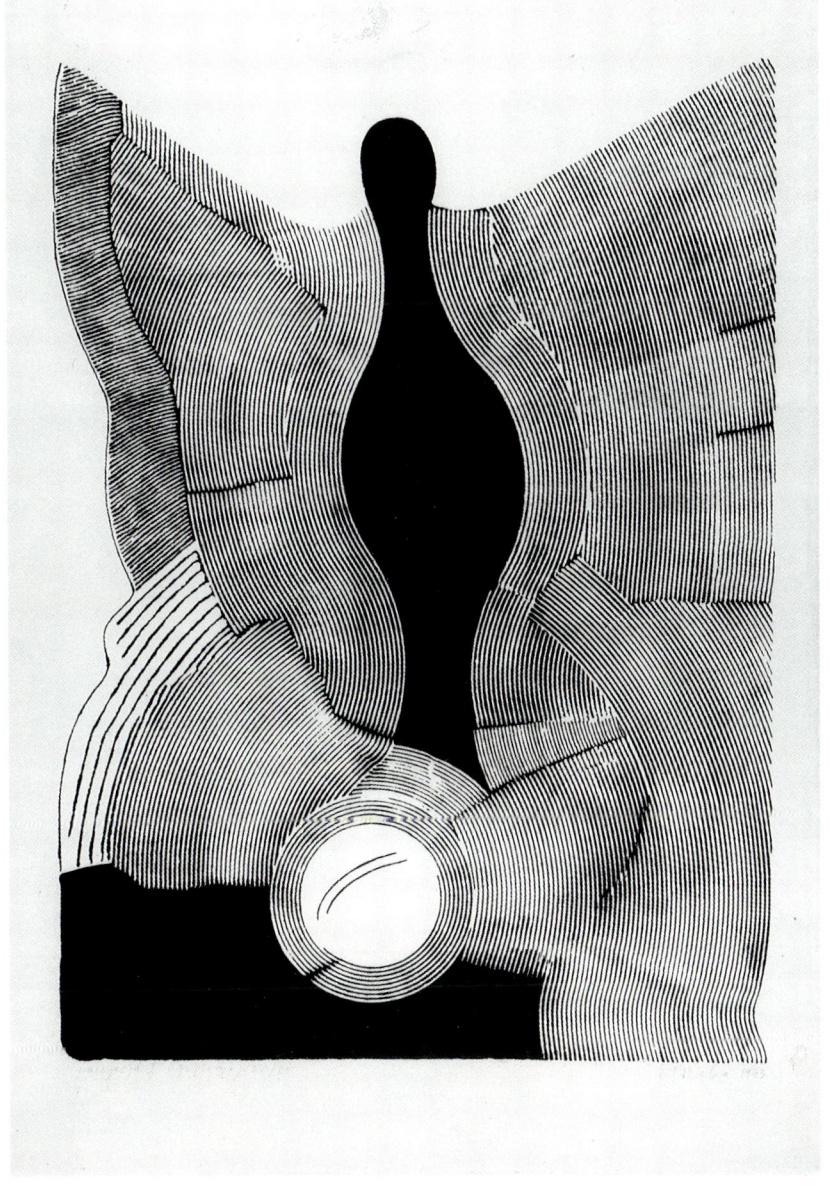

You might like to experiment with the process yourself. A photocopy will reproduce an identical picture mechanically. A photocopy of a suitably enlarged photograph would be ideal. You could use a self-portrait. Overdraw the picture. Start with five or six to get the simple clichés out of the way! After these you will have disposed of all the easy solutions and will have to really think to develop an interesting new image. Perhaps you could imagine developing the character rather than just the expression.

Ryszard Otreba (b. 1932), Initiation 1, 1973, one of a series of 16 prints based on letters to his wife, plaster print, 75.5 × 56 cm, Tate Gallery, London.

The Work Process

SURFACE OR RELIEF PRINTS

The Japanese woodcut (opposite) is a relief print. The print is made from the raised surface of the woodblock. Any area that is not required is therefore cut away. Each colour was usually printed from a separate block. The most difficult problem to solve was, therefore, making sure that the areas of colour fitted together perfectly. This was usually based on the first, or 'key' print, which established the black outlines so characteristic of the Japanese woodblock print. Ordinary commercial plywood can be used to create a woodblock print. Large areas of surface are easily removed with a sharp knife or a broad chisel. Complex designs may be created using this technique. In some cases designs with up to 16 different printings, and therefore colours, were produced.

The limitations of this technique were often its strengths, since bold areas of single colours created simple images of great power. These were influential in the late 19th century when prints started to become available in Europe. Artists like Manet and Van Gogh collected the often failed prints that arrived in packing chests of Japanese imports. You can find examples of these treasured prints in the backgrounds of the painters' works. Can you find out which ones?

You might like to collect objects which have interesting surface patterns or textures. You could assemble these to form a printing block. To do this you would have to ensure that all the surfaces you wished to print in each colour were raised to the same level. You could print multicoloured prints by giving each of the objects you have collected a different printing.

Pablo Picasso (1881–1973), Still Life Under Lamp, *1962, coloured lino cut, 52 × 64.5 cm, Museum of Modern Art, New York.*

Ito Shinsui, Girl Washing Linen, 1917, *woodblock print, British Museum, London.*

Without the disadvantages that the woodgrain can give, as seen in Japanese woodcuts, lino is a useful and underrated material. It will cut more sympathetically if sharp tools are used and if the lino is warmed before cutting. Working on lino has frequently been used in schools as an easy and convenient way to produce a simple block print. It is often seen as a technique that can only print a simple image. It is a relief printing technique that has much in common with the Japanese woodcut.

In this print by Picasso (left) all the colours were printed from one block. The design on paper was first transferred to the lino surface. If you try it you may find carbon paper will help you to do this. All the areas he wished to remain white he cut from the block, and then he printed the whole edition in the lightest colour so that the next printing would cover unwanted areas. He then cut from the block all the areas he wished to remain the first colour and printed a second colour. This process was repeated until the print was fully coloured.

Relief prints can be made from any raised surface, so the two techniques described here are only examples.

Printmaking should be as flexible an approach to art as any other technique. You should not feel bound to rules or fixed sequences of events. The techniques should be used to direct, rather than rule, the work you produce. Lino and woodblock prints can place large areas of colour next to one another. For the student, a practical number of colours is three to five. Obviously as you gain experience you will learn how to use more colours. Drawings for this type of printing therefore need to go through a design stage in order to work out how the colours can be fitted together.

From a series of objective drawings create a design that you feel will print well. It will help you to examine these illustrations, and any others you can find. From this study you will gain a knowledge of what the technique will do well and what your design should avoid. Picasso used a strong light source to help simplify his still life designs. Perhaps you could experiment with strong light sources in a similar way.

INTAGLIO PRINTS

The three examples on these pages are examples of prints produced as part of a series. Find out what you can about the series to which these examples belong. The stories that lie behind them are a fascinating insight into the uses to which printmaking has been put through the ages.

Rembrandt van Rjin (1609–1669), The Presentation at the Temple, *c. 1654, etching and drypoint, British Museum, London.*

Make a series of quick drawings concentrating on line. You might like to look at the 'Los Caprichos' series and reflect on modern images which might update the story. This would be working in the same way that Hockney used to update the original 'Rake's Progress' story. Use the best of your drawings to develop an etching. Remember, the print can be developed after printing as well as on the plate.

Etching, drypoint and engraving are all 'intaglio' methods of printmaking. They are worked on a hard surface. Though glass and plastic can be etched, metal is usually used in drypoint and engraving. Wood engraving is a technique that uses the end grain of hard wood. (An example of a wood engraving can be seen on page 2.)

The techniques of drypoint and engraving print from lines scratched or cut into a metal plate. Care and practice are required when you do this since errors are difficult to burnish out. To cut into a metal plate requires hard metal tools and strength, and of course great care since the tools can easily slip on the metal surface and cut you.

In etching, the lines are cut into the plate by the action of acid. Lines to be etched are first scratched through a protective layer, a ground, of an acid resistant waxy substance. Little effort is required by the etcher since the acid does all the hard work. Intaglio printmaking techniques print from the cut or etched areas. It is the direct opposite of surface printing since the surfaces are wiped clean of any ink; the ink used to print remains in the cut lines.

All these are essentially line techniques. To achieve tones, areas of grey, lines are frequently drawn close together or across each other to create denser areas. Tones can also be created by making many tiny dots. This is known as stippling.

In the two prints, by Hockney (below left) and Goya (below right), a technique for producing tones called aquatint is used. This needs an acid bath. It creates tone through stopping the acid from eating some parts of the plate by melting spots of resin onto the plate. The areas not coated, and therefore eaten into by the acid, hold the ink and print a tone. Different tones can be created by covering the plate with differing amounts of resin.

David Hockney (b. 1937), Bedlam, *from 'A Rake's Progress', 1961/63, etching and aquatint, Tate Gallery, London.*

Francisco Goya (1746–1828), The Sleep of Reason Produces Monsters, *from the 'Los Caprichos' series of etchings and aquatints, British Museum, London.*

The fluidity of drawing through a ground applied to a metal plate is an exciting experience. Waiting until the etched plate is removed from the acid adds to the expectation. Printing shows if you have achieved your aim. Perhaps the nearest you can come to the experience, and a good way to prepare for it, is to draw with a biro pen. Though it is a poor substitute it has one thing in common which you can get used to – it can't be rubbed out and therefore changes must be drawn in.

Andy Warhol (1928–1989),
Marilyn Diptych, 1962, *acrylic on canvas, 205.4 × 144.7 cm, Tate Gallery, London.*

Of all the printmaking processes available, screenprinting is probably the most common one to be found in schools. It is a versatile medium which uses the basic idea of stencilling to good effect. The screenprinter uses large wooden frames covered with a fine woven cloth. Organdie used to be quite common but now very fine, often synthetic, meshes are woven especially with screenprinting in mind. Inks are forced through the cloth with a hard rubber blade called a squeegee. The screen must be in contact with the paper to be printed.

The design is created by blocking out various parts of the screen, so that no ink can get through. The screen can be blocked with simple paper stencils or with special film stencils that can be ironed onto the mesh. It can be drawn on with wax or painted on with specialised fillers or varnish. It can be blocked with photostencils as in the Warhol above. Of course, the artist can use a combination of all these. Usually a screen is devoted to each colour, since each requires a different stencil. From the prints here the repetitive possibilities of the process can be seen.

In the print by Andy Warhol (below) the image has been repeated to create a wall of flowers. To make the variety greater the colours of the individual flowers have been changed. The print eventually covered the interior walls of a whole room. Warhol developed a whole series of screenprinted canvases. In these he repeated the same image many times. You might like to find out what you can about the work of this artist, especially his repeated images. Do you think repetition increases the effect of the simple image?

Andy Warhol (1928–1989), Flowers, 1964, 304 × 304 cm each, silkscreen on canvas, part of one wall of an exhibition at Leo Castelli Gallery, New York.

Screenprinting can also be useful as the first stage in a more complex work. Quite often it can form the background colour to other art forms. Embroidery can be based on the broad areas of colour laid down by a screenprint. Screenprints can be drawn into before, during and after the printing process. You might like to produce a piece of fabric-based work which develops the shapes and colours laid down by printing from a screen. You could produce the print by brushing varnish onto the screen. This will give a broken image which will need all your skill to develop.

You could produce a flower wall of your own, or indeed any other large environmental work. Make sure you get permission to use the space first! Screens could be used to decorate a large area, after all this is frequently done with wallpaper or printed fabric. You would need to prepare well, perhaps even make scale drawings so that you can calculate the number of screens and their position.

Looking at Graphic Design

GOTHIC	ABCDEFG Old English	abcdefghijk
OLD FACE	ABCDEFGH Bembo	abcdefghijkl
TRANSITIONAL	ABCDEFGH Baskerville Old Face	abcdefghijk
MODERN FACE	ABCDEFGH Bodoni	abcdefghijkl
EGYPTIAN	ABCDEFGH Rockwell	abcdefghij
FAT FACE	ABCDEFG Carousel	abcdefghij
SANS SERIF	ABCDEFGH Helvetica	abcdefghijkl

Some common letter forms.

LETTER SHAPES

The ability to use the written word is an essential part of the graphic designer's work. A knowledge of typography is therefore very important; typography is the art of designing printed texts.

The twenty-six letters of our alphabet are capable of an inexhaustible series of different combinations. We call these combinations words and the rules that order them are, of course, the rules of spelling. When we read we are in direct communication with the author. Thought of in these terms the alphabet is a remarkable tool.

Though the general letter shapes are set, the proportions of the letters and the way each letter stroke ends are often variable. Letters can be tall and thin or short and fat, the only limitations occur when the letter becomes unreadable. The ends of the letters are often finished by a stroke called a serif. This helps the letters run together as you read along a line of printed text. Letters can also finish with a flourish in imitation of old-fashioned copperplate handwriting. Letters without either are called sans serif, like the text you are reading.

The main types of letter forms are shown above. The basic letter shapes have developed over thousands of years, yet the designs often still bear the marks of the original writing tools. The differences in the weight of the lines in the Gothic alphabet, for example, refer back to the way the pen was used in the original hand-lettered manuscripts.

Though the basic letter shape is set there are a wide variety of shapes and designs to choose from. It is important for a designer to have some knowledge of this variety since choosing the appropriate typeface is an important part of the designer's task.

The vast majority of advertisements are set in one of these five typefaces:

Futura
Franklin Gothic
Bembo
Garamond
Goudy

g g g g g

Test the truth of this by making a survey of the advertisements that appear in one periodical magazine. To help you identify each typeface you could look for the shape of the small letter (or lower case) 'g' as this is very distinctive.

The catalogues produced by such companies as Letraset show the wide variety of letter forms that are available. Typefaces fall into two basic categories, display and text faces. Display faces are the most numerous category. These are used for titles, headlines and other eye-catching uses as in the photograph. Quite frequently these are invented for a specific purpose.

Large blocks of words are printed in text, or book, faces. Fewer of these are available and the basic requirement of this sort of face is legibility. This is always limited by the average reader's ability to cope with unusual patterns of type. Since legibility is the most important aim, the typographer tries to make the text as simple to read as possible. The standard text faces have been used for many years. In the front of some textbooks you will see which typefaces have been used. Check through your books, you will soon find you come across the same typefaces again and again.

Desktop publishing programs enable typefaces and sizes to be manipulated simply and different alternatives tried out before a solution is chosen. This would have been difficult in the days before computers were common. Computers are a useful tool and aid to the solution of design problems, but they should not be seen as providing the only answer or to limit the imagination of the designer.

You might like to look through a variety of magazines to see how different typefaces are used. Can you find examples where you think the designer has made a particularly good or bad choice? Explain why you think this is so.

Variety

The grid below gives a small indication of the number and variety of commercially available typefaces. This type of letter shape is not usually set as a a page of text but is often used by typographers for headings and titles. In addition to commercially available typefaces the designer can adapt typefaces by hand or even design whole alphabets for a particular function. Increasingly this can be done by computer programs.

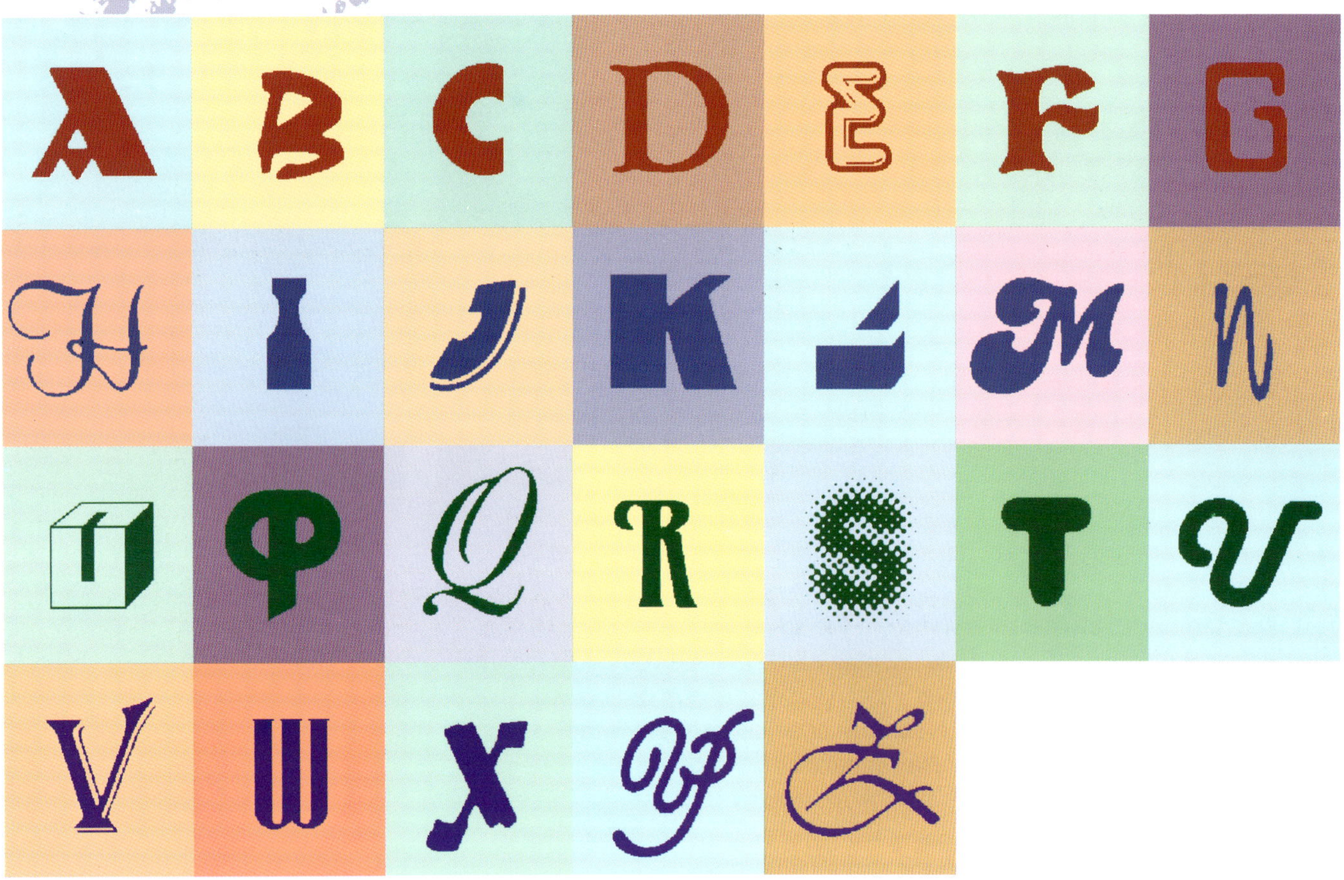

A selection of the many typefaces available from Letraset.

Dan X. Solo's Explosion alphabet.

The Explosion alphabet (above) is one of those designed by Dan X. Solo. Also in his catalogue are alphabets called Chinatown, Comic Book, Computer, Dracula and Driftwood. What do you think they look like? Choose one of these titles and produce an alphabet of your own design.

Some display faces that have been designed to convey a particular idea.

Above are some examples of display letters that have been designed for a particular purpose. Perhaps you could suggest the names of some imaginary companies that might use them? Collect examples of display letters that have been designed in this way.

This sign (right) is placed in one of the most beautiful areas in the country. It uses local materials that are in harmony with the woodland surroundings. Investigate some local materials in your area that might be suitable for a similar situation. Try to design structures that do not look out of place. Find a local beauty spot or a place of historical interest. Make a survey of the way signs are used there. Perhaps you could interview those responsible. Suggest ways in which the signposting could be improved. You might even design and construct an example.

This use of texture in a letter shape (below) comes from a well known product. It reflects the nature of the product. Do you think the letter design would be as successful if the letters were in solid black? Can you collect other examples of the use of texture to enhance the letter shape?

Sign from a National Park in Cumbria.

The specially designed logo for the Aero chocolate bar.

Sources of Lettering

In order to understand the part that the printed word plays in our lives you need to get out and about and look. We are so used to lettering in the outside world that we have stopped really looking at it. We are so used to the printed word in the context of books and magazines that we do not realise the effect that scale, colour, position and typeface can have on our world.

Local planning authorities often go to a lot of trouble to ensure that shop signs or outdoor advertising fits in with its area without being too visually intrusive. We only really notice this when a sign slips through their net and we are forced to look at something hopelessly out of sympathy with its surroundings. Can you find an example of this from your local area?

Once you start to look you will be amazed at the variety of display faces that are used. Here are some suggestions for collecting examples of letter shapes:

- *Shop signs.* Make a study of the lettering used in shop signs in your area. Divide your collection into categories. You might like to list the hand-painted or the three-dimensional signs as groups. Can you make a photographic record of the more unusual letters? You could find out how the preformed or illuminated signs are made. Perhaps you could talk to a signwriter and find out how they work.

Jenny Holzer (b.1950), Selections from The Survival Series, 1987, Barbara Gladstone Gallery, New York.

This work is by an artist who uses lettering as an 'installation'. This example was situated in Showplace Square in San Francisco. The lit letters were placed in an appropriate environment to express her ideas. Illuminated letters are often found giving information; here the technique has been used creatively.

- *Graveyards*. Macabre, but interesting! Look at the way fashions in letter shapes have changed down the centuries. Find out how the mason carves an inscription; you might be able to watch one at work. Look at carved letters on war memorials and public buildings. Make a collection by drawing, taking photographs or, if you ask the church authorities, by wax rubbing some interesting individual letters.
- *The printed word*. Collect examples of display type from magazines and newspapers. If you limit the sources of your material you could study it in some depth. An interesting place to start might be to choose some special publications, such as fashion or teen magazines for example. Consider the way lettering is used in packaging. You might like to collect letter forms from a single source like tin labels or sweet wrappers.

No doubt you can find many other areas of study to give you the same sort of wide-ranging collection. This will be of value when you need to find letter forms for your own design work.

The shop below has a fascia, the decorated shop front, well suited for a busy modern shopping centre but how well would it fit into your high street? Do you think it would fit into an old-fashioned village or town centre?

Eye-catching typography has been well used on this shop front.

You could draw from life some examples of shop fronts which are sympathetic to their settings and some which are not. You could try and define those elements that make or prevent them fitting into place. Try to find an example that does not fit and suggest ways that it might be redesigned to be more sympathetic to its surroundings. Pay particular attention to the way lettering has been used, or misused. You could present your suggestions in drawn or modelled form.

Imagine you have come to this country from abroad and that you know no English. How helpful are shop signs, for example, if you cannot read the language? Do certain types of shop have a style that is recognisable above the complications of language?

Signs and Symbols

Rockfish, illustrated map showing how the Romans penetrated ancient Britain.

Information graphics give two main types of information. Quantitative graphics give facts, statistics and precise measurements. They aim to give information to the informed non-specialist and specialist alike. They give this information as accurately as possible. In graph form the axes of the graphs are usually defined so that they can be readily understood. Frequently this type of graphics is produced by computer.

Non-quantitative graphics are often directed at the lay person with little or no background knowledge, and aim to give an impression or show a trend. The example above gives a clear indication of how Celtic Britain was taken over by the Romans. It is visually clear and far more interesting to look at than a straightforward table of dates and place names.

Information graphics form a large part of the graphic designer's work. You only have to look at one of the quality Sunday papers to see how often information graphics are used to make complex issues more easily understood. You might like to collect from newspapers, textbooks etc., examples of both good and bad examples of this sort of design work. Can you find an example that works really well and identify why it is so successful? Can you find an example that actually gives a false impression or makes the information more difficult to find? Try to suggest ways it could be improved.

School textbooks are often full of information presented graphically and there are plenty of examples of good and bad practice. Use your skill as a designer to replace some of the worst examples. Mount a copy of the original and your replacement next to each other and try to explain why yours is better.

Computers come into their own when presenting information in this way and they put high quality design outcomes within everyone's reach – everyone who has the imagination to use them creatively. The computer graphic (below) can be printed out, turned on an axis, rescaled, etc. in ways unimaginable to designers who only use paper. However, even with this technology, it still requires the basic clarity necessary in less dramatic paper designs. The best technology cannot make a bad design good.

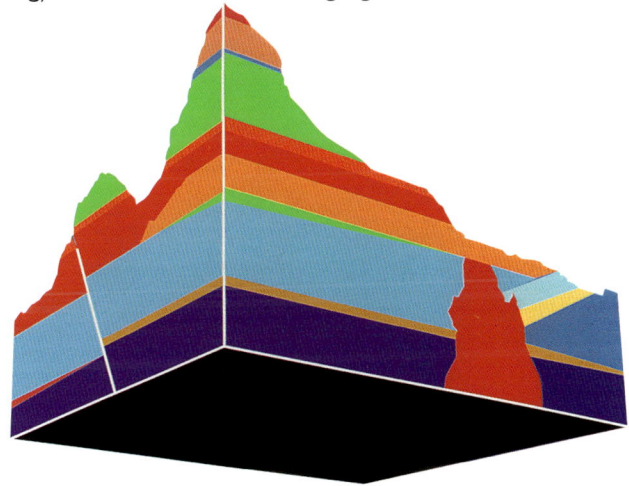

Computer graphics image of a three-dimensional, coloured model of a geological cross-section

Airbrushed cut-away diagrams of the human body.

These diagrams help to explain to the non-specialist the workings of the human body. They are far simpler than the medical illustration on page 29. The non-specialist would have little trouble understanding these.

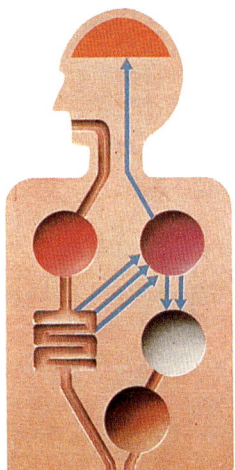

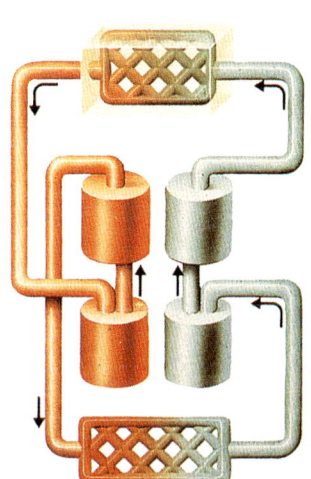

We are used to reading the shorthand of signs. Most people are so familiar with road traffic signs, for example, that they are read, understood and acted upon without conscious thought. These signs are the result of careful design. More complex signs can be designed and, as can be seen on these pages, they do not have to be boring or abstract.

Otl Aicher, pictograms for the town of Isny, Germany, 1981.

Find other signs, not necessarily road signs, which have conventionally agreed meanings. Can you identify signs which give a clue to their meaning by the symbols they use? The pictograms above are a clear example of this. The one on the left was designed for a nature trail to give information in a clear way. Could you design pictograms for a similar purpose around your home area?

The concept sheet below shows how two simple symbols were developed. They were for a book on gardening and they stand for the idea of building, in this case walls, paths etc., and cultivation. The symbols developed are sufficiently close to the activities they refer to that they can be readily understood without reference to a key. Frequently, however, signs only have a meaning because we agree they will have that meaning. It is a convention that a red circle with a white horizontal bar in it means 'no entry'.

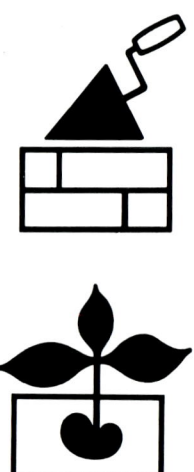

Simon Jennings, sketch concept and final designs for 'cultivation' and 'construction'.

You might like to develop a method of working using concept sheets like the one opposite to record all your ideas – even the duds! This entry (below) is from a brochure describing bed and breakfast accommodation in Kent. Can you identify all the symbols used? Write down those you can understand without the key. Choose three of those you think you recognise and redesign them to make them clearer.

SOUTHBOROUGH
Mrs Barbara Ingram-Monk
The Nightingales
London Road, Southborough
R. Tunbridge Wells TN4 0UJ
Tel: (0892) 528443
Fax: (0892) 511376

1 ¹/₂ m S of Tonbridge
⇌ Tonbridge

Map ref: D2

Grade II listed house only two minutes from A21 with fast access to M25. Bedrooms have tea/coffee making facilities and colour TV. Bathroom with shower. Extra toilet. Double room has hand basin. Garden and parking. Extensive breakfast menu.
Bedrooms: 1 single, 1 double, 1 triple/family
Prices: single £15, double £30, triple/family £30-£40
Reduced rates for children over 5, groups, over 60's and longer stays.
Open all year except Christmas and New Year.

Accommodation guides often use simple graphic symbols to describe facilities instead of using words.

These signs (below and on page 23) were produced to help give the companies they represent a visual identity. This helps them stand out from their competitors. The signs (called logos when used in this way) are part of the house style that can be extended via a design manual to every aspect of the companies' operation. You might like to design a logo for your own use. It might help identify all your work and establish a 'house style' of your own.

Logos for The Royal Bank of Scotland and El Al Israel Airlines.

Designing for Advertising

There are many different vehicles for advertising. Television is the most obvious but because it is outside the reach of most companies, especially local small businesses, it is not the most common. You might like to make a list of all the different types you can think of. In the example (left), by skillful drawing and a modern characterisation – note the trainers – the artist has produced an interesting and memorable image from a simple and unpromising subject. Can you make a mouthwash look interesting?

Advertisers have always appreciated the effect that unusual media can have on the message. The Goodyear airship floated above sporting occasions for many years. It was known to millions even if not associated immediately with car tyres. The beer bottle van dates from the 1920s while hot air balloons float above our countryside in a wide variety of shapes. These forms are called fringe media.

The two examples below show that the only limit to choice of media is the imagination of the designers who use it. You might try to design a balloon to advertise an appropriate product of your own choice or, based on a suitable photograph from a car magazine, redesign some vehicle into an advertisement. Perhaps you can think of a medium that has not yet been used; you might be the first to recognise its potential, after all someone had to think of the two examples here.

Colin Brown, advertisement for Pepsodent.

Daimler bottle van, 1924, The National Motor Museum, Beaulieu.

These two examples show the variety of unusual media available to the advertiser. In each case it is the medium that is eye-catching, not the message.

Not all advertisers feel the need for the extremes of fringe media. The poster is, and has been for a long time, a very powerful medium. This poster (above) was a part of a campaign designed by the agency Leo Burnett. They play on the French associations of the company's product – bottled water (*eau* in French). With a small budget they have created and captured the market for their product.

The example, *Picasseau*, is presented in a Cubist style. Perhaps you could try to design a poster using these masters' work. If you look up their style as painters it will help you:

> Miro
> Watteau
> Murillo
> Canaletto
> Michelangelo
> Tintoretto

If you think this use of fine artists' work is unusual in advertising then try to make a study. See how often artists' work is used. The better your knowledge of art history is, the better your chances of finding some.

Illustration

RESEARCH

Perhaps closest in feeling to the work of the fine artist is the work of the illustrator. In many cases the illustrator has a style or method of working which is drawn to the attention of Art Directors, either through publications in which the illustrator can pay to be represented, or by the simple expedient of hauling a portfolio around the offices of any likely client. Illustrators often become known for a certain style and presentation of work. This can become fashionable and much sort after. To reach acceptance, however, a well researched, well presented portfolio is required. As an illustrator starts off this may be entirely made up of college work, though today colleges try to give students the chance to include accomplished works in their portfolio. They do this by arranging commissions while the student is still at college or by entry to competitions. As you progress, college work is often replaced by successful commissions. As your work and your reliability become well known, commissions should become more frequent, if they don't you don't eat!

Jane Bennett, Kittens and butterfly.

The work of a freelance illustrator can be financially very difficult in early years. It is important that your portfolio is of the highest quality; if it's not getting you work, find out why and improve it. Students need to accept the value of constant refinement in their portfolios and continually research new techniques and subject matter. Even successful illustrators need to keep work under review.

Working with animals needs constant practice and study. The cats drawn here are an example of work on a subject well known and studied. If you wish to work at this level you need to work hard with your subject, often over a period of months or years. You might find examples of this type of project that have been published as they stand. Clearly considerable commitment is needed, you need to love your subject.

The page of a student's drawings illustrate the lively mind that should always be at work in a sketchbook. These pages support a project based on the idea of a kitchen garden, half in existence today, half remembered. As a starting point, before any image was fixed, the student made a drawn record of all that she thought might relate to her chosen subject. Sorting out the image came later.

You might like to accept the challenge to make a visual diary or sketchbook of a certain part of your garden, or a part of a local park. Plants, insects, visiting birds and fungi all have a part to play in your record.

Often this method of sorting out the content of a picture works well for the artist, for it is inclusive and gives unexpected scope to the subject. The trick for the artist is not to let the finished product appear like a shopping list.

Student's sketch work.

MEDIA

These two examples have been chosen to show that illustrations are not always paper-based, that the media used can be as wide as those used by other artists. The quality of technical reproduction techniques means that there are few limitations on the media used. The 3D work, for example, is presented to the client as 5×4 inch transparencies. These mean that the complexities of handling 3D media can be allowed for by the artist who also takes the pictures. The correct lighting, for example, worked out by the illustrator becomes a part of the illustration. In the case of *Portrait of Isaac Newton* the classical façade, the scientific equipment and the real apples allow the artist to pass on the information that the brief requires in an interesting and challenging way. It is this transferring of information according to a preset brief that makes illustration the tool of the graphic designer and not a work of painting or sculpture. The actual form, the way the idea is presented, is close to the work of the artist Joseph Cornell. It is Jon Hamilton's intention to communicate a preset message that separates the works.

Jon Hamilton, Portrait of Isaac Newton, *to illustrate Newton's discovery of gravity for the* New Scientist *magazine, mixed media.*

Liz Sanders was set a clearly predefined brief in her work (below), one that even laid down the media to be used. The brief was to construct an image reminiscent of a breakfast cereal packet (but not resembling any particular packaging). The illustration was to be entirely assembled using a wide range of cereals and shows how precise a brief can be. The resultant work shows how creatively an imaginative artist can respond. After all, many great paintings were produced for clients who had very clear ideas of the contents they wanted to find in the work they commissioned, yet the artist, by controlling the form in which the work has been presented, has managed to create original work. The illustrator need not be highly specialised in one particular medium. To be versatile and imaginative is a talent that has a place of its own in the illustration market.

You might like to choose a letter from a children's alphabet book and then develop it in a medium of your own, devising an illustration for it. Try to develop a medium which reflects the subject you have chosen to help the child identify the letter. Your alphabet could have a theme, for example nautical – A is for anchor, B is for boathook, etc.; food – A is for anchovy, B is for bacon, etc.; animals – A is for aardvark, B is for bison, etc.

Liz Sanders, Breakfast Time, *commissioned as a magazine cover by the Consumer's Association, breakfast cereals and glue on board.*

Technical Illustration

The technical illustrator may require a deeper understanding of the subject than many other illustrators. The main purpose is often to explain highly technical details, and this is very difficult if the illustrator has little concept of the technology being explained. Technical illustrators often work on workshop manuals, explaining the way pieces of machinery fit together.

Perhaps you can get hold of a car maintenance manual. Often there are drawings of parts of machinery that cannot actually be seen but have to be visualised by the illustrator. The illustration (left) is a cut-away drawing showing all the parts of a watch. Clearly the illustrator has had to use considerable skill and powers of invention to complete this drawing. The drawing would have been impossible unless the artist understood the workings of the watch and could decide which parts were important and which could be safely hidden. All this may sound a bit daunting, but in fact there are various conventions and skills that can be learnt to aid the process.

For an illustrator who is interested in this type of work there are many college courses that give all the basic training required, but it is clear from the examples here that a very good drawing ability is required to start with. A certain ability with drawing instruments is also required. Though the technical illustrator is not a draughtsperson he or she certainly has to be able to read technical drawings and to work from them.

You might like to start your career with the 5 amp plug or some similar common piece of technology – keep it simple though, your efforts to illustrate the inside of a school computer might not be appreciated! Take the plug apart and then, through your illustrations, show how it could be correctly reassembled. Test your skill as an illustrator by asking someone to follow your instructions literally. Be careful to get someone who knows about electricity to check the wiring before the plug is used!

Leonardo da Vinci produced illustrations of many of his inventions. These have recently been constructed from his drawings. The accuracy of his drawings is shown by the ease with which drawn ideas could be translated into actual products. Technical accuracy is of prime importance, though not at the expense of clarity. The medical illustration (right) contains an enormous amount of information and, though it needs effort to follow, nowhere does the complicated labelling interfere with the information shown. Medical textbooks would be impossible without this kind of illustration. This is a highly specialised form of technical drawing. The artist responsible for this illustration is in fact a doctor and it would be hard to imagine this type of work without some experience of dissection.

John Harwood, cut-away watch, *airbrushed magazine illustration.*

Collect examples of the work of technical illustrators. You will be surprised at the number of uses that their work is put to. Can you find examples of their work from the past?

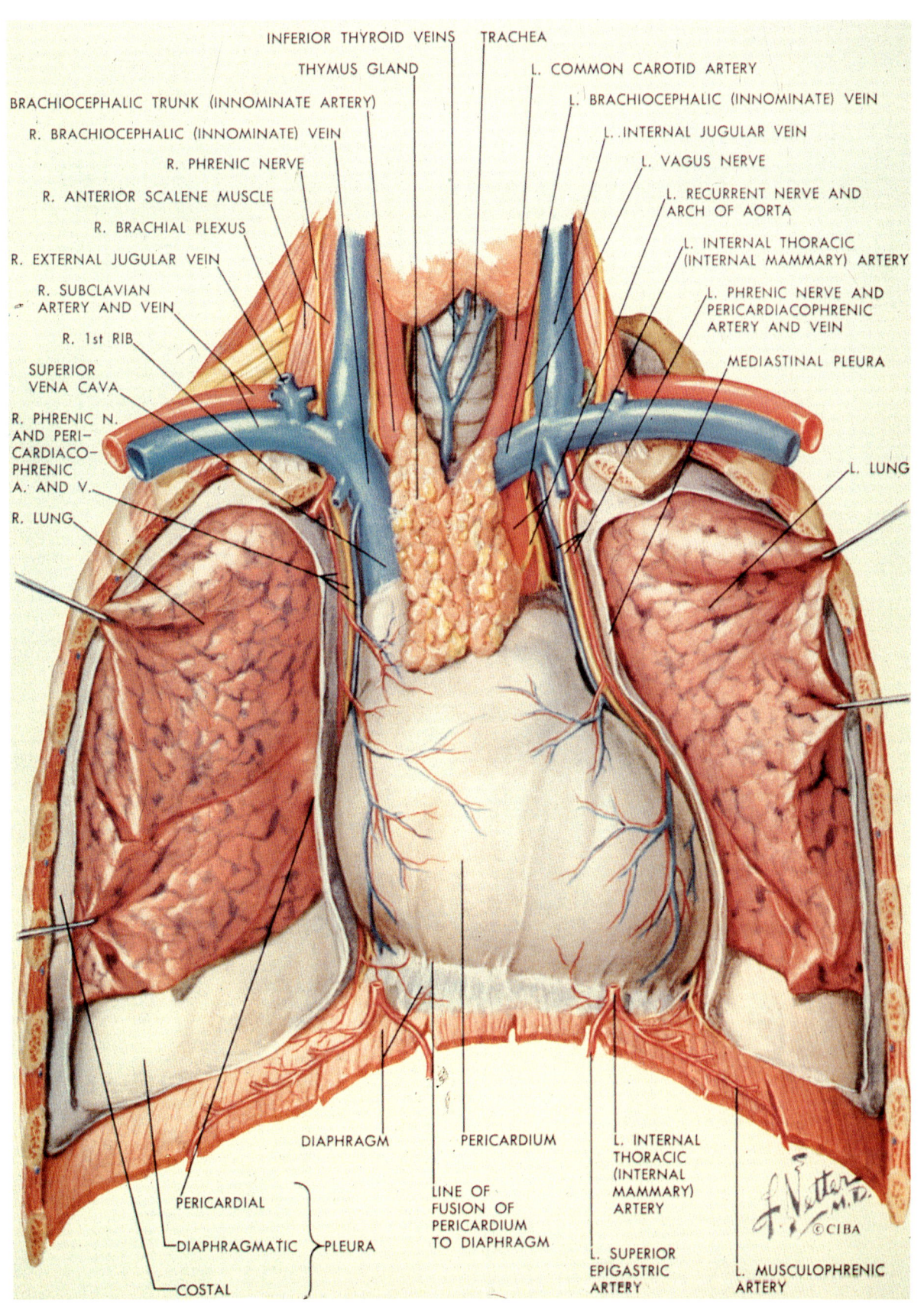

INFERIOR THYROID VEINS — TRACHEA

THYMUS GLAND

L. COMMON CAROTID ARTERY

BRACHIOCEPHALIC TRUNK (INNOMINATE ARTERY)

L. BRACHIOCEPHALIC (INNOMINATE) VEIN

R. BRACHIOCEPHALIC (INNOMINATE) VEIN

L. INTERNAL JUGULAR VEIN

R. PHRENIC NERVE

L. VAGUS NERVE

R. ANTERIOR SCALENE MUSCLE

L. RECURRENT NERVE AND ARCH OF AORTA

R. BRACHIAL PLEXUS

L. INTERNAL THORACIC (INTERNAL MAMMARY) ARTERY

R. EXTERNAL JUGULAR VEIN

R. SUBCLAVIAN ARTERY AND VEIN

L. PHRENIC NERVE AND PERICARDIACOPHRENIC ARTERY AND VEIN

R. 1st RIB

MEDIASTINAL PLEURA

SUPERIOR VENA CAVA

R. PHRENIC N. AND PERI-CARDIACO-PHRENIC A. AND V.

L. LUNG

R. LUNG

DIAPHRAGM — PERICARDIUM

L. INTERNAL THORACIC (INTERNAL MAMMARY) ARTERY

PERICARDIAL

LINE OF FUSION OF PERICARDIUM TO DIAPHRAGM

DIAPHRAGMATIC ⎫ PLEURA

L. SUPERIOR EPIGASTRIC ARTERY

COSTAL

L. MUSCULOPHRENIC ARTERY

Frank Netter, medical illustration for Ciba.

𝒩 ETWORK

This book covers two very diverse areas of graphic art; printmaking and graphic design.

PRINTMAKING

Printmaking lists the various techniques available with the names of some of the most famous artists who have used these techniques. The prints which they produce, usually for more general sale than their other artworks, are more readily available since they were produced by the artist in quite large numbers. There was always the temptation for artists to produce many of the more popular images to make more money.

Artists often produced prints in self-defence, since particularly successful pictures were often reproduced in print form by inferior artists. Artists quickly recognised printmaking as an art form of its own, with its own strengths and weaknesses. William Blake is a clear British example of this.

TYPOGRAPHY

Typography is the basic material of communication design since letter forms are universal to all who share a language. Originally typefaces were made from cut wooden shapes and, later, cast lead. Now most manipulation of letter forms takes place on the computer screen with complex graphics packages that can select, often from vast lists, letter size and shape. Using facilities like 'mirror', 'rotate' and 'skew' and the addition of perspective lines, the letters can be reshaped to suit any designer's requirements.

A selection of letters designed by Dan X. Solo.

ILLUSTRATION

Illustration is the graphic area closest to the work of painters and sculptors. While all use visual images, the illustration is used to convey information. Its context is purely commercial.

   The art of illustration is an ancient one, the most easily seen examples are the medieval illuminated letters or the Books of Hours. A good example is *Les Tres Riches Heures de Duc du Berry* by the Limburg brothers. The illustrations here show the Dukes' castles on the pages representing the months of the year. With the advent of printed books many artists, using the print media of the day – woodcuts and wood engravings – made book illustrations. Look at the work of Albrecht Durer. The work of Aubrey Beardsley and Norman Rockwell also deserves attention.

Doffy Weir, from 'There's a Monster in my House', to illustrate a line of text – 'She gets paint in her hair', *commissioned by Collins Educational in watercolour.*

For Dianne and Serena.

ACKNOWLEDGEMENTS

Cover and title page illustration: *Thames Valley* poster, courtesy of the Science and Society Picture Library.

Special thanks are due to the following artists who provided copies of their work and permission to reproduce them:

Jane Bennett (24); Jon Hamilton (26); Colin Brown (22 top); John Harwood (28); Hilary Paynter (2); Rockfish (18); Doffy Weir (31).

The author and publishers would like to thank the following individuals, institutions and companies who have given permission to reproduce photographs and artwork in this book. Every effort has been made to trace and acknowledge ownership of copyright. The publishers would be glad to make suitable arrangements with any copyright holder whom it has not been possible to contact.

Advertising Standards Authority (23 right); Aero Logo Trademark owned by and reproduced with the permission of Société des Produits Nestlé SA, Vevey, Switzerland (15 bottom left); courtesy Barbara Gladstone Gallery, New York (16); Bartle Bogle Hegarty (3 both right); British Museum, London (7, 8, 9 right); El Al Israel Airlines (21 bottom); Frank Netter © Ciba, Collection of Medical Illustrations volume 5 Heart, reproduced by Ciba-Geigy plc, Basle, all rights reserved (29); with thanks to the Heart of Kent Consortium (21 top); Leo Castelli Gallery, New York © ARS, NY and DACS, London 1995 (11); Mike Feeney (Red Herring Design and Illustration) (12, 13 left, 14 both, 15 both top, 31); Museum of Modern Art, New York © DACS 1995 (6); The National Motor Museum, Beaulieu (22 bottom left); Perrier UK Limited (23 left); Photographer: Liz Sanders, reproduced by kind permission of Consumers' Association (27); Precision Visuals International/Science Photo Library (19 top); Quarto Publishing plc/Simon Jennings (19 all bottom, 20 bottom); with the kind permission of The Royal Bank of Scotland plc (21 middle); Stadt Isny/Allgäu (20 both top); Tate Gallery, London (3 left, 4, 5); Tate Gallery, London © David Hockney (9 left); Tate Gallery, London © ARS, NY and DACS, London 1995 (10); Window on The World™ Photo Library © David Usill/Photographer (22 bottom right).

A catalogue record for this title is available from the British Library.

ISBN 0 340 627220

First published 1995
Impression number   10 9 8 7 6 5 4 3 2
Year   1998   1997

Copyright © 1995 Chris Dunn

Typeset by Wearset, Boldon, Tyne and Wear.
Printed in Hong Kong for Hodder & Stoughton Educational, a division of Hodder Headline PLC, 338 Euston Road, London NW1 3BH by Colorcraft Ltd.